Valorie Quesenberry

Everyday Moments with God

Prayers for Women

D0167089

BARBOUR BOOKS
An Imprint of Barbour Publishing, Inc.

© 2012 by Barbour Publishing, Inc.

ISBN 978-1-63409-132-9

eBook Editions:
Adobe Digital Edition (.epub) 978-1-60742-578-6
Kindle and MobiPocket Edition (.prc) 978-1-60742-579-3

Published by Barbour Books, an imprint of Barbour Publishing, Inc., P.O. Box 719, Uhrichsville, Ohio 44683, www.barbourbooks.com

Our mission is to publish and distribute inspirational products offering exceptional value and biblical encouragement to the masses.

 Member of the
Evangelical Christian
Publishers Association

Printed in the United States of America.

CONTENTS

Prayer is our lifeline to God. As my relationship with Christ has deepened through my life, I have come to realize what an amazing resource prayer is.

I was blessed to have parents who believed in praying about everything and audibly thanking God when He answered. Because of their example, it has seemed natural to me to take all the moments of my life—the joys, sorrows, panic, grief, triumph, and praise—to Him as well.

In this book, you will find everyday prayers—the kind we women pray as we encounter daily life. I hope you will be inspired and challenged to rely on our heavenly Father in any and every situation. It will make all the difference in your day.

Cheers and Celebrations

PRAISES

*"Now thank we all our God,
with heart and hands and voices,
who wondrous things has done,
in whom this world rejoices."*

Martin Rinkart

THE ONE WHO IS

Heavenly Father, today I'm grateful for all You are—the God who is, the God of the living, the great I Am. Your character is unchanging. You are the epitome of perfect holiness and love. Because of who and all You are, I believe and trust in You. Your truthfulness is indisputable and Your power is established. Not just for the majestic works by Your hand but for the pure glory of Your nature—I worship You today. Amen.

Who is like the Lord
our God, who dwells on high?
PSALM 113:5 NKJV

GRACE FOR EVERYTHING

Father, I'm thankful for Your *grace*—Your unmerited favor to me through Jesus Christ, and that special strength You give Your children in times of need, trial, and temptation. If not for Your grace, I wouldn't even be able to approach You. Thank You for extending favor to me: forgiving my sins and adopting me into Your family. And thank You so much for that extra dose of perseverance that You keep giving to me in tough situations. I'm so thankful Your resource center will never experience a shortage. I praise You today for grace. Amen.

But he gives us more grace.
JAMES 4:6 NIV

AMAZING FORGIVENESS

Lord, I come into Your presence, thanking You for forgiveness. In a culture where many experience clinical depression because of guilt, I can know my past is redeemed because of Christ's sacrifice for me. Your forgiveness is so amazing. Although I don't deserve it, You pour it out freely and lovingly. Because You have seen fit to pardon me, I bless Your name today.

In Him we have redemption through His blood, the forgiveness of sins, according to the riches of His grace.
EPHESIANS 1:7 NKJV

PROVISIONS FROM GOD

God, there is no creature on earth You do not see or provide for. I'm bringing praise to You right now for the daily things You supply for me. It is through Your goodness that I have food to eat, clothes to wear, and water to drink. Help me always to be thankful for what I have and to not emulate the wandering Israelites who, focusing on lack, preferred to complain. Your power is awesome; thank You for generously supplying my needs and wants each and every day.

You open Your hand and satisfy
the desire of every living thing.
PSALM 145:16 NKJV

NONE LIKE YOU

God, when I consider my own inadequacies, I am amazed at Your perfectness. You are truth and justice, holiness and integrity. There is none like You. You are the One and only true God. Other deities disappoint their followers; other idols fail. But You never do. Because You are perfect holiness, all Your other attributes are only good. There is no selfishness, vengefulness, or deceitfulness in You, Lord. Thus, I can trust You completely and revel in Your light unafraid. Amen.

"No one is holy like the LORD, for there is none besides You, nor is there any rock like our God."
1 SAMUEL 2:2 NKJV

THE INSPIRATIONAL WORD

Lord, Your Word thrills me, convicts me, comforts me, and strengthens me. I am so thankful that You gave us the Bible. Thank You for inspiring the prophets of old as they penned Your truth. Thank You for protecting the scripture through centuries of skepticism and persecution. Thank You for giving me the blessing of this treasure, for allowing me to hold it in my hand. When I am hungry, Your Word feeds me; when I am fearful, it assures me; when I am uncertain, it guides me. Your Book is the light upon my path. Without it, I would be lost. Amen.

All Scripture is God-breathed and is useful for teaching, rebuking, correcting and training in righteousness.
2 TIMOTHY 3:16 NIV

DIVERSE GIFTS

Dear God, today the fellowship of other believers ministered to me. There are times when I get frustrated with the Church—it has its challenges. But so does a human body. And yet when each bodily organ serves the function for which it was made, there is life, energy, and passion. Help me remember, Lord, that You made my spiritual brothers and sisters with diverse gifts; help me work with them, not against them. Thank You for reminding me again today this family of God is one of Your treasures, a blessing from Your hand—and heart. Amen.

There are different kinds of gifts,
but the same Spirit distributes them.
1 CORINTHIANS 12:4 NIV

TO EVERY GENERATION

Jehovah God, I come just now to revel in Your faithfulness. From generations past to this very minute, multitudes have testified that You always come through. Yet there have been times in my life when I thought You had overlooked me, that You weren't aware of my needs, that You didn't hear my prayers. But my doubts proved false, and Your record is untarnished. You didn't promise that I would always understand Your ways, but You did promise Your presence and love in every circumstance. And I can testify it's true. I love You, Lord. Amen.

Your faithfulness endures to all generations.
PSALM 119:90 NKJV

THE GIFT OF SALVATION

Dear Father, thank You for the gift of salvation, for sending Your only Son to be a sacrifice for all people, even those who didn't want Him. I am in awe of Your mercy extended to me. It is incredible to think that I am a daughter of God. Thank You, Jesus: You didn't walk away from the cross, but You laid down Your life for me. Thank You, Holy Spirit, for drawing me to this greatest of gifts. My life is forever changed. In Christ's name, amen.

For the grace of God has appeared that offers salvation to all people.
TITUS 2:11 NIV

THE PAST IS GONE

Father, I'm glad You have redeemed my past. I've said and done things of which I'm not proud. I'm grateful that You've blotted out my sins and given me a fresh start. Like one using a marker board, You wiped away the shame and guilt and handed the marker back to me. I don't have to live in the past; I can face the future with confidence and grace. In Christ's name, amen.

As far as the east is from the west, so far has He removed our transgressions from us.
PSALM 103:12 NKJV

A FATHER

God, help me remember that You're my Father. A heavenly Father—One who has unlimited resources and power and One who has infinitely more love than any great earthly dad. When Satan tempts me to view You with suspicion, help me remember that his goal is my utter destruction. Lord, fill my heart with the truth that You love me perfectly and have only the best in mind for me. In fact, You want to embrace me, bless me, and give me heaven as my inheritance. What a wonderful Father You are! Amen.

As a father has compassion on his children, so the LORD has compassion on those who fear him.
PSALM 103:13 NIV

Of Earthen Jars

HEALTH

*We ourselves are like fragile clay jars
containing this great treasure.*

2 Corinthians 4:7 NLT

COMMON COLD?

Dear Lord, I feel miserable. I've got a cold, and it feels anything but common. I don't know which of the many strains this is, but my head is full of pressure, my throat raw, my nose red, and my eyes watery. I'll have to keep a tissue box and throat lozenges handy today. Help me through this day, Lord. Although this cold is not a serious trauma, it is extremely unpleasant, and I just need to know someone cares. And thank You that colds typically have a 100 percent recovery rate! Amen.

You can throw the whole weight of your anxieties upon him, for you are his personal concern.
1 PETER 5:7 PHILLIPS

DENTAL VISITS

Thank You, God, for dentists. Although I wouldn't want to spend my days with my hands poked into other peoples' mouths, I'm sure glad they do. I'm grateful for braces, dentures, crowns, and bridges. Thank You for fillings and for Novocain when I need them. If I'd lived a hundred years ago, my dental experiences would no doubt be much more traumatic. So, though I hate sitting helpless in that chair, thank You that I have a good dentist. And, please, don't let him hit a nerve today! Amen.

(A Psalm for Dentists):
Open your mouth wide, and I will fill it.
PSALM 81:10 NLT

A GOOD PATIENT

God, I'm off today for my annual mammogram. I confess it's not my favorite part of being a woman. In fact, I don't feel very charitable toward Eve right now—that bite of fruit sure means discomfort for me today! I don't look forward to my breasts being squeezed and squished by a machine, but I'm thankful that You've allowed the medical world to discover technology that detects potential problems early. I place the results of today's screening in Your hands. Now, please help me be a good (and cooperative!) patient. Amen.

Trust in the Lord with all your heart, and lean not on your own understanding.
Proverbs 3:5 NKJV

VISION

God, I'm so grateful for advances in corrective lenses! Whatever the problem—nearsightedness, farsightedness, astigmatism, etc.—there is help today for those with deficient vision. If I'd lived a hundred years ago, I'd have worn coke-bottle glasses! I'm so glad for all the choices available in the twenty-first century. I know You've allowed technological advances for greater reasons than my vanity, but I'm thankful anyway. It is a blessing to be able to see! Amen.

The hearing ear and the seeing eye,
the Lord has made them both.
PROVERBS 20:12 NKJV

COMPLETE SURRENDER

Lord, I'm scared. I am scheduled for a medical test soon. I know my body is temporal and made of dust, but I truly don't want there to be something wrong with it physically. Yet help me surrender to what You have decided for me. Still, I'm earthly. . .and seen from my perspective, the situation is really frightening. Show me how to trust You minute by minute—not in the hope that everything will be as I want, but in the certainty that You've thought of every angle of my life and You are in control of all the details. Amen.

When I am afraid,
I put my trust in you.
PSALM 56:3 NIV

WAITING. . .AND WONDERING

God, I'm scheduled for a biopsy. Wow,
those words scare me! It means there's
a possibility that something horrible
could be growing inside me. I don't like
needles or incisions or waiting for the
results—that's the worst part, the waiting.
And the wondering. I just want this to
be over and in the past. So I guess I just
need courage today, Lord. And some
comfort, too. This is one of those times
when I'm so incredibly glad I have a
heavenly Father to whom I can turn. Just
get me through this, please. Amen.

*"My grace is enough for you: for where
there is weakness, my power is
shown the more completely."*
2 CORINTHIANS 12:9 PHILLIPS

WAITING ROOMS

Dear Jesus, someone I love dearly is in the hospital. I'm sitting here in the busy waiting room, watching for the doctor, wanting news, and yet dreading to hear it. Others surround me, connected to this place by a person they care about. We're people from every stratum and season of life with one thing in common—knowing someone who is suffering physically. Lord, illness and injury have to obey Your will, and so do the emotions that burden the hearts of those here. Please visit every waiting area and patient's room, and bring the cure that only comes from You—tranquility, mercy, and courage. Amen.

Now the God of peace be with you all.
ROMANS 15:33 NKJV

A PERFECT PLACE

Creator God, I wish there weren't diseases in our world. Those tiny microbes that infiltrate the immune system are responsible for so much pain and grief. Although sickness was not present in the Garden of Eden—that perfect place You intended for us—it is a part of this life now, a consequence of the curse under which our world suffers. But someday You'll create a new earth, and I know bacteria won't stand a chance there. I look forward to that, Father God, for then the world will once again be "very good." Amen.

Now I saw a new heaven and a new earth, for the first heaven and the first earth had passed away.
REVELATION 21:1 NKJV

INTERNAL CLOCKS

Heavenly Father, it seems like every person has an internal rhythm seemingly permanently set to a certain time in the day. There are early birds and night owls and middle-of-the-day people. Not many of us are successful in changing our internal clock, Lord. Maybe You wanted to create humans with varying peak hours of energy. It would be a pretty boring world if we all fizzled out at the same time each day. Thank You for the variety You have provided in all of us. Amen.

To declare Your lovingkindness in the morning, and Your faithfulness every night.
PSALM 92:2 NKJV

FITNESS

It's an exercise-crazy world we live in, Lord. Gym memberships are prized, morning jogs are eulogized, and workout clothing has become a fashion statement. There are some who make this area of self-care too important; they spend an inordinate amount of time on it. Yet others don't keep it high enough on their priority list. Help me, God, to keep the proper perspective of fitness, because, after all, I have a responsibility for the upkeep on this body. It's on loan from You. Amen.

Bodily fitness has a certain value, but spiritual fitness is essential both for this present life and for the life to come.
1 TIMOTHY 4:8 PHILLIPS

Dear Lord, the transition of minutes to hours is so incremental that it is tedious to observe. It's much easier to focus on a large chunk of time than a myriad of tiny ones. Yet hours are made up of minutes, just like the body is comprised of cells. Each is vital to the whole. Lord, help me remember that each minute of the day is a small section, a slice of my life. Help me make the best use of every minute. Amen.

Make the best use of your time, despite all the difficulties of these days.
EPHESIANS 5:16 PHILLIPS

Our Daily Bread

PETITIONS

Give us this day our daily bread.

MATTHEW 6:11 KJV

A JOB FOR ME

Dear heavenly Father, I need a job. You know the challenges I'm facing in my present situation. You understand the reasons why I need to make this change. There are so many people looking for work; employers have a large pool from which to draw. Still, You've promised to supply my basic needs if I would keep Your kingdom top priority in my life. So, I ask that You would direct my search and help me approach this transition with integrity and consideration for my present employer. I ask this in Your name, amen.

"But seek first the kingdom of God and His righteousness, and all these things shall be added to you."
MATTHEW 6:33 NKJV

GETTING STARTED

Dear Lord, the first step toward any goal is the hardest, and I just don't feel motivated to take it. But there are things I need to do, and so far I haven't found a fairy to do them for me. Procrastination is a terrible hindrance. I know. I'm a closet procrastinator. I don't like to admit to it, but You see it anyway. Thank You for giving me more chances than I deserve. Remind me that I just need to start. Inspiration often springs from soil watered with obedience. Let me learn this lesson well. Amen.

The way of the sluggard is blocked with thorns.
PROVERBS 15:19 NIV

EMPLOYER WOES

God, I have the most demanding boss ever. I need to demonstrate the love of Christ, but it can be challenging when my superior is, at times, so hard to please. Give me courage, Lord, to rise above my emotions. Help me to pray for my boss as the Bible tells me to and to serve as though it is an assignment from You. For You, Lord, are my true superior. Bless my boss today, God, and show Your love to him through me. Amen.

Whatever you do, work at it with all your heart, as working for the Lord, not for human masters.
COLOSSIANS 3:23 NIV

DIFFICULT PEOPLE

Dear Lord, I ask You to help me be patient and kind today. The Bible speaks about longsuffering. That's what I need as I deal with difficult people and irritating situations. Whether it's squabbling children or rude drivers or harried clerks, I know there will be those today who will irk me. In those moments when I want to scream, help me remember to forbear and forgive. It's just so easy to react, but help me instead to deliberately choose my response. I'm depending on Your power, Father. Amen.

*Bear with each other and forgive
one another if any of you has
a grievance against someone.*
COLOSSIANS 3:13 NIV

UNLIMITED RESOURCES

Father, the Bible says You own "the cattle on a thousand hills." You have unlimited resources. So I'm asking You to supply a special need I have today. Although I try to be a good steward of the money You give me, some unexpected event has caught me without the necessary funds. I know You can remedy this situation, if You deem that good for me. Because You're my Father, I'm asking for Your financial advice. I need Your wisdom in this area of my life. Amen.

"For every animal of the forest is mine, and the cattle on a thousand hills."
PSALM 50:10 NIV

"'The silver is mine, and the gold is mine,' declares the LORD Almighty."
HAGGAI 2:8 NIV

LOST!

Lord, I've lost my cell phone again!
Please help me find it! I know sometimes
I'm careless; help me learn from this. But,
Lord, You know how much information is
in that phone and how much I need it to
carry out my responsibilities today. You
know where it is right now. Help me think
of that place. Guide me to it. And just
like the woman with the lost coin—I will
rejoice! Amen.

> *"'Rejoice with me, for I have
> found the piece which I lost!'"*
> LUKE 15:9 NKJV

GOD IS A SHIELD

Protector God, today I'm remembering someone in the armed forces. Though I know war wasn't in Your original plan for this world, it has become a necessary tool for overcoming evil. The Bible recounts stories of You leading Your people, the Israelites, into battle to defend what was right. So there is honor in defending freedom and justice. I ask You to protect this one from danger; dispatch Your peace, and put a hedge before, behind, and around him. Watch over all those who are putting their lives in harm's way for my sake. In Christ's name, amen.

He shields all who take refuge in him.... He trains my hands for battle; my arms can bend a bow of bronze. You make your saving help my shield.
PSALM 18:30, 34-35 NIV

COMMUNICATION

Dear God, the Internet is a marvelous tool! Thank You for giving humankind the ability to invent it. But the Internet also has a great potential for evil. I ask You to protect my family from online predators, from sexual content, from sites that would have a negative influence on our relationship with You. Help me to be prudent in my use of the web. Like any other means of communication, it can be used wrongly. But, with Your help, it can be an instrument for good in our home. Amen.

*I will set nothing wicked
before my eyes.*
PSALM 101:3 NKJV

A SHINING LIGHT

Dear God, I want to be a better witness for You. I have friends and family members who don't know You, and every day I interact with people who aren't believers. Lord, I don't want to be corny or pushy, but I do want to let my light shine before others. I ask You to open up the doors for me today. Let me sense Your prompting. And let the silent witness of my life also speak to others about Your great plan of salvation. In Jesus' name, amen.

"Let your light so shine before men, that they may see your good works and glorify your Father in heaven."
MATTHEW 5:16 NKJV

Home and Family

RELATIONSHIPS

O Lord, our God, our homes are Thine forever! We trust to Thee their problems, toil, and care.

BARBARA B. HART,
"A CHRISTIAN HOME"

BLESS MY HUSBAND

Father, thank You for creating marriage. You knew we would need its structure and blessing. My husband enriches my life in so many ways. And he has a lot of responsibility before You for our marriage. I ask You to give him strength for his role as spiritual leader in our home. You made him courageous and bold, but Satan, who doesn't want my husband to succeed in leading our family toward spiritual understanding, knows how to work against us. Defeat Satan today, I pray. Let my husband assume his responsibility with strength and joy. In Christ's name, amen.

"It is not good for the man to be alone."
GENESIS 2:18 NLT

STILL LEARNING

Lord, I'm really ticked at my husband right now. I just don't get it. How can he be unaware of how his insensitive words hurt me? What I really want to do is quote all those Bible verses to him— the ones that say "love your wives" and "be not bitter" (Colossians 3:19 KJV). But I know You're the only one who can really speak to his heart. Please open his understanding to the way words affect me as a woman. Teach him how to be gentle. And help me remember I'm also a student in relationships. May we both let You control the classroom! Amen.

Above all, love each other deeply, because love covers over a multitude of sins.
1 PETER 4:8 NIV

I BLEW IT

Lord, I blew it today. I was unkind to my husband and harsh with my kids. I wish I could take back my attitude and words. Sometimes it's difficult for me to understand why You still love me. I am so thankful You would trust me with a family, even though I've done a pretty terrible job of nurturing today. Please forgive me. Your Word promises me cleansing if I confess. Help me to remember this the next time I feel frustrated and impatient. Help me exercise my will and choose to respond appropriately to the family You've given me. In Christ's name, amen.

If we confess our sins, He is faithful and just to forgive us our sins and to cleanse us from all unrighteousness.
1 JOHN 1:9 NKJV

KEEP ME

Dear Father, in the scurry of life, I often forget to be thankful for important things. So many times You've shielded my family from physical harm, and I didn't know it until later. And I'm sure I don't even know about all those moments when You've guarded us from spiritual danger. Although we are the apple of Your eye, I realize we're not immune to trauma and disaster; You won't remove the effects of the curse until the right time comes. But for now, I'm grateful that You care about us and that the only way something can touch us is after it's passed Your gentle inspection. Amen.

*Keep me as the apple of the eye,
hide me under the shadow of thy wings.*
PSALM 17:8 KJV

SIBLING REVELRY

Heavenly Father, thank You for my siblings. When the chips are really down, I can depend on them. They know my background, my temperament, and my journey. We share the same blood and the same basic life philosophy. When we were kids, we squabbled a lot; but now, I just love getting a call from one of them. They understand me like no one else. And I pray we'll always be there for one another. Bless my brothers and sisters today. In Jesus' name, amen.

Whoever claims to love God yet hates a brother or sister is a liar. For whoever does not love their brother and sister, whom they have seen, cannot love God, whom they have not seen.
1 JOHN 4:20 NIV

ROLE REVERSAL

Dear Lord, when I was growing up, my parents seemed ageless. But I realize now that my time with them is getting shorter every day. They're getting older, Lord; and, more and more, I find myself looking out for them. This role reversal is really difficult for me. I'm accustomed to them looking out for me, and part of me wishes I could stay in their care for a while longer. Please give me strength to deal with this new phase of our relationship, and help me to honor them as long as they live and beyond. Amen.

"Even to your old age, I am He, and even to gray hairs I will carry you! I have made, and I will bear; even I will carry, and will deliver you."
ISAIAH 46:4 NKJV

CHERISH

Dear God, thank You for sending a strong man to love me. He is strong not only in physical strength but in his emotional and mental stability. I don't want that to change, but I ask You to help him learn the language of tenderness. I understand it's hard for a man to grasp what affection and gentle words mean to a woman, but I ask You to help my husband learn how to cherish me verbally. And there may be some significant need in his life that I am not meeting—give me insight, and let me make his happiness my goal. Amen.

Love knows no limit to its endurance, no end to its trust, no fading of its hope; it can outlast anything.
1 CORINTHIANS 13:7 PHILLIPS

MIDLIFE EMOTIONS

Help, Lord! I'm married to a man in midlife crisis! I'm not sure whether to cry with him or ignore him. He is measuring his life by what he has accomplished— his job status, his assets, his reputation. I measure my life by my relationships—the state of my marriage, how my children are maturing, and the friendships I enjoy. So, God, please help him in ways I can't. Override his fears with Your peace and infuse him with the certainty of his great value, regardless of the goals he hasn't yet reached. I love him, with or without hair! Amen.

May the God of hope fill you with all joy and peace as you trust in him, so that you may overflow with hope by the power of the Holy Spirit.
ROMANS 15:13 NIV

Dear Lord, this communication thing is not working. How can my husband and I resolve conflict and work for unity when we don't even speak the same language? When I'm trying to explain something, he hears things I don't even say. And when he talks. . .well, okay, he doesn't talk much. But when he does respond, I don't get it. He thinks I'm illogical, and I think he's insensitive. It really does complicate things. Help me hear what my husband is really saying and not jump in with a quick response. Give us both an attitude of love the next time we talk. In Jesus' name, amen.

If I speak in the tongues of men or of angels, but do have not love, I am only a resounding gong or a clanging cymbal.
1 CORINTHIANS 13:1 NIV

THE ONLY ONE FOR ME

God, You brought my husband and me together out of the billions of people on the planet. I valued him above any other guy around. I couldn't wait to be his wife. And I think he felt the same about me. After several years of marriage, the grind of daily living and the imperfections and oddities we see in each other sometimes make us blind to the gifts of the other. Today, help me remember what a great guy my husband really is, and open my eyes to the things that made me fall in love with him in the first place. Amen.

How handsome you are, my beloved!
Oh, how charming!
SONG OF SOLOMON 1:16 NIV

CONFLICT

Dear Lord, my husband and I had an argument today. The marriage experts tell us that conflict is unavoidable and normal. It's how we resolve it that counts. But I'm not sure we scored very highly in that regard. Both of us are still upset. So help us to process this conflict correctly and get beyond it. Usually, our disagreements begin over something silly anyway. Help us to value our marriage more than our individual rights. Help me to let it go and welcome him home tonight. In Jesus' name, amen.

If you are angry, be sure that it is not out of wounded pride or bad temper. Never go to bed angry—don't give the devil that sort of foothold.
EPHESIANS 4:27 PHILLIPS

DELIGHT IN HONORING HIM

God, I want to be the wife my husband needs in every area of our lives. You created him with a deep need for respect, which greatly influences his contentment level, his ability to succeed at work, and his attitude toward me. Let me not just meet the "requirements," but rather, let me take joy in meeting his needs. I ask You to give me the desire and the wisdom I need to bless my husband in this way. Amen.

Love each other with genuine affection, and take delight in honoring each other.
ROMANS 12:10 NLT

A CHANNEL OF CARE

Lord, I'm living in the sandwich generation. I have grandkids on one side and aging parents on the other. When I'm not babysitting preschoolers, I'm caring for the elderly. And there are diapers involved in both jobs. I'm glad I have the health and resources to bless my parents who have done so much for me all their lives. And I wouldn't trade these sweet years with my grandchildren for anything. But, all the same, sometimes my emotional fund feels overdrawn. I need extra strength and peace today, Jesus. Let me be a channel of care to those I love. Amen.

"Come to Me, all you who labor and are heavy laden, and I will give you rest."
MATTHEW 11:28 NKJV

Higher Ground

GOALS

"Lord, lift me up and let me stand,
By faith on Heaven's table land;
A higher plane than I have found;
Lord, plant my feet on higher ground."

JOHNSON OATMAN JR.,
"HIGHER GROUND"

SPIRITUAL GUARDRAILS

Dear God, help me to erect proper boundaries in my life. I don't want to fall prey to a sin simply because I wasn't being careful. Just like guardrails on a dangerous mountain highway, boundaries in my life keep me closer to the center and farther away from the cliffs. I know Satan is plotting my destruction, but Your power is greater. Let me cooperate with Your grace by a careful lifestyle and a discerning spirit. In Christ's name, amen.

Stay alert! Watch out for your great enemy, the devil. He prowls around like a roaring lion, looking for someone to devour.
1 PETER 5:8 NLT

PASSION AND PURPOSE

Father, I'm in a rut. I like some familiarity, but this monotony is wearing away at my sense of purpose. I know there are parts of our lives that are not particularly glamorous, fulfilling, or significant (at least, on the surface). Yet living without passion or purpose isn't what You had in mind for us. Show me, Lord, how to find meaning in my everyday life. Open up my eyes to the subtle nuances of joy folded into life's mundane hours. I put my longings into Your hands. Amen.

In Him also we have obtained an inheritance, being predestined according to the purpose of Him who works all things according to the counsel of His will.
EPHESIANS 1:11 NKJV

CHEERFULNESS

Jesus, I can't imagine You as a sour, solemn man. I believe You enjoyed life immensely, and I know You brought joy to those around You. Why else would "sinners and tax collectors" want to eat with You (as Your enemies pointed out)? Your mission on this planet was sacred and grave; but I believe Your demeanor in everyday life was buoyant and pleasant. Others loved being in Your presence. Help me pattern my daily attitude after Your example and take heed of Your command to "be of good cheer." Let me reflect You by the way I approach living. Amen.

"Be of good cheer, daughter."
MATTHEW 9:22 NKJV

PEOPLE AT THE TOP

Dear God, I need help with my priorities.
It is so easy for them to get out of whack.
Show me the things I've let creep to the
top that don't belong there. Point out to
me those areas where I need to put more
emphasis and commitment. Lord, let me
remember that people are worth more
than possessions and pursuits. Let my
unseen checklist of priorities reflect that.
Amen.

*"For wherever your treasure is,
you may be certain that your
heart will be there too!"*
MATTHEW 6:21 PHILLIPS

QUIET AND GENTLE

God, I read in Your Word that You value spirits that are gentle and quiet. At times, this is oh so hard for me, Lord! I'm not a total pushover, but I do have my own opinions about things. Sometimes it is so hard to keep quiet or speak softly. Yet, Lord, You know that I want to be that way. The universe has enough bossy women. Teach me, Lord, how to be quiet and gentle. Amen.

The unfading beauty of a gentle and quiet spirit...is of great worth in God's sight.
1 PETER 3:4 NIV

A QUIET QUEST

Dear Lord, we all find great blessings when in community with others, enjoying those times when we are with people. But I need Your help to embrace solitude, too. Let me see the value in spending some time alone, giving my mind time to decompress, refreshing my spirit in the quiet. Not only do I need to spend quiet time with You in personal worship, but also I need to incorporate into my daily routine those pockets of time when the music is off and the computer is down. Help me make times of quiet my quest. Amen.

"In quietness and confidence shall be your strength."
ISAIAH 30:15 NKJV

BLESSED ARE THE FLEXIBLE

Flexibility is a struggle for me, God. I don't like interruptions in my routine. It's challenging for me to accept a rerouting of my day. Still, sometimes, You have to reorganize for me, because I haven't recognized Your promptings. Or maybe there's someone You need me to meet or a disaster You want me to avoid. Help me to accept the detours in my plan today, aware of Your sovereignty over all. Amen.

This is the day the LORD has made;
we will rejoice and be glad in it.
PSALM 118:24 NKJV

TRUE HOMELAND PERSPECTIVE

God, I want to live with an eternal perspective. Heaven is more than a feel-good fable for the graveside. It's an actual place, as real as this earth and far more lasting. When I live like this earth is the ultimate goal, I tend toward selfish indulgence. When I remember that heaven is my real destination, I put value on the lasting things, the things of true importance. Remind me to keep an eye toward Your heavenly kingdom. Amen.

They freely admitted that they lived on this earth as exiles and foreigners. Men who say that mean, of course, that their eyes are fixed upon their true home-land.
HEBREWS 11:13-14 PHILLIPS

JUST DO IT

Dear Lord, I want to have an obedient heart. Sometimes, when You speak to me, I feel hesitation or want to postpone what You're telling me to do. Yet that means either I don't trust You or I want my own way, neither of which is good. A child ought to obey her parents because she acknowledges their right to direct her and because she trusts the love behind the words. Help me, Lord, to embrace that kind of attitude when You speak to me. In Christ's name, amen.

But be doers of the word, and not hearers only, deceiving yourselves.
JAMES 1:22 NKJV

WORRY? NOT!

Dear Lord, Your Word tells me it is wrong to worry. I try to tell myself that it's only concern, but actually, that's putting a nice spin on the issue. Older women used to say that females are just born worriers. I guess there's some truth to that, maybe because we're so invested in relationships, and most of our worrying is about those we love and care for. Still, You know worry isn't good for us and it doesn't accomplish anything. So, today, help me not to worry, but to turn all my "concerns" over to You.

Don't worry over anything whatever; tell God every detail of your needs in earnest and thankful prayer, and the peace of God which transcends human understanding, will keep constant guard over your hearts and minds as they rest in Christ Jesus.
PHILIPPIANS 4:6-7 PHILLIPS

THE SIMPLE LIFE

Dear God, *simplicity* is a buzzword today. It seems everyone wants "simple" in some fashion. Perhaps it's because life has become too complicated for many of us; we yearn for a more laid-back lifestyle. Lord, I need to simplify my goals in my relationships and my work. Doing so will help me to have a more laserlike focus. And in my spiritual life, a little simplifying might be good, too. Instead of daily reading numerous chapters of Your Word, help me to concentrate on one or two verses, thus deepening my understanding of You. Lord, help me keep simple goals and a simple faith as I simply live for You. Amen.

Aspire to lead a quiet life,
to mind your own business,
and to work with your own hands.
1 THESSALONIANS 4:11 NKJV

THE PATH TO JOY

Lord, I live in a culture that demands more. Wherever I look, I see glossy advertising of things I "need." It's difficult to be content when you're bombarded with messages to the contrary. But I know that accumulating more stuff isn't the path to joy. And You don't bless me so I can indulge myself, but so I can share with others. Let my life be marked by restraint and a deep contentment that's rooted in You, the center of my fulfillment. In Jesus' name, amen.

Keep your lives free from the lust for money: be content with what you have.
HEBREWS 13:5 PHILLIPS

TIME MANAGEMENT

Dear God, sometimes I think I need more than twenty-four hours in my day! It seems I never have enough time. I think with longing about simpler seasons in my life when I could actually complete my to-do lists. There was such satisfaction in having a few stress-free moments. Now, my schedule is filled, and I'm so harried. Holy Spirit, please guide me in this area of my life. How I use my time is part of stewardship, so I'm asking for Your wisdom. Show me how to manage the hours I have so I can honor You in everything I do. In Christ's name, amen.

Teach us to number our days,
that we may gain a heart of wisdom.
PSALM 90:12 NIV

MEEKNESS

Heavenly Father, I want to develop the characteristic of meekness, a kind of quiet strength. Rather than a sign of a pushover, meekness is a trait of the strong. It takes guts to be silent when you want to speak. Meekness is not a goal for the weak of heart. It is, rather, for those who would be in the forefront of spiritual growth. Like Moses, the meekest man on earth (see Numbers 12:3), we can reap the rewards of quiet strength in our lives. Amen.

With all lowliness and meekness, with longsuffering, forbearing one another in love.
EPHESIANS 4:2 KJV

BACK TO CENTER

Heavenly Father, I need balance in my life. It's one of the hardest things for humans to achieve. We're so prone to lopsidedness, to extremes. Maintaining center is challenging. That's why I need You to straighten me out and help me stay in the narrow way. In those areas of my life where I'm listing to the side, bring me back to center, O Lord. In Jesus' name, amen.

Don't wander away from the path but forge steadily onward. On the right path the limping foot recovers strength and does not collapse.
HEBREWS 12:13 PHILLIPS

Cocoons and Wings

MOTHERHOOD

To every thing there is a season.
ECCLESIASTES 3:1 KJV

NEW BABIES

Heavenly Father, thank You for our new baby. You've blessed our home with a new life to nurture and guide. I'm overwhelmed with the responsibility and overcome with joy. I'm trying to adjust to the fact that I'm really a mother! I'm afraid I can't do this. Maybe I won't be a good mother. And it seems I'll never get back on a normal schedule or get a good night's sleep! But, God, I'm trusting You to help me with this huge task. As helpless as this baby is without me is as helpless as I am without You. Thank You, God, for being my Father and allowing me to mother my precious little one. Amen.

He. . .will gently lead those
that have their young.
ISAIAH 40:11 AMP

LEGACY

Dear God, what kind of legacy am I leaving? I want to be remembered as more than a woman who dressed nicely, had a great family, and went to church. I want to be remembered for the way I invested myself in the lives of others. After all, love is the only lasting thing on this earth, something that will remain when I am physically gone but living with You in eternity. Lord, let my legacy be wrapped up in serving others in love. In Jesus' name, amen.

Prophecy and speaking in unknown languages and special knowledge will become useless. But love will last forever!
1 CORINTHIANS 13:8 NLT

Father, give me wisdom today to discipline my children. This motherhood job requires skills beyond my natural capabilities. When I remember that I'm training the next generation of adults, I almost panic. Will I be able to equip them to handle life? Well, not in my wisdom alone, but You can fill in the gaps left by my human limitations. I want to discipline them in a way that teaches them to respond well to authority yet does not crush their spirits. Help me discern the difference between childish immaturity and outright defiance. I'm depending on Your guidance as I raise the children You placed in my care. Amen.

*The rod and reproof give wisdom,
but a child left undisciplined
brings his mother to shame.*
PROVERBS 29:15 AMP

FOR THE PRODIGALS

Heavenly Father, I'm asking You to be with my children tonight. Like prodigal sons, they are in a far country. They are focused on the world and making choices accordingly. It's as if they have forgotten about who You really are. I want so desperately to intervene, but You keep reminding me to pray much and talk little. Right now, Lord, demonstrate Your power and Your love for them in ways they can't ignore. Bring them back to Your path. In Christ's name, amen.

Let him return to the LORD, and He will have mercy on him; and to our God, for He will abundantly pardon.
ISAIAH 55:7 NKJV

FOR YOUR GLORY

Lord, thank You for my children and their uniqueness. You've blessed them with individual gifts and abilities. As they grow, Father, show me how to help them discover their full potential. You didn't give any of us our talents that we might use them to indulge our own pleasures, but to bring glory to You and blessings to others. Let me guide my children as they look toward the future, and may they someday be contributing, godly adults who honor You. Amen.

I have no greater joy than to hear that my children walk in truth.
3 JOHN 1:4 KJV

DAUGHTERS

Lord, You've given me a daughter to love and raise. Thank You for trusting me with her. I want her to mature into a beautiful, confident, godly young woman. I pray that she will reflect the example I've set and will value the things I do. Help me portray womanhood in a positive and biblical way. Show me how to direct her to Your principles in decisions of attitude, dress, and relationships. Teach me how to be the mother she needs so someday she can be the woman You had in mind when You created her. In Christ's name, amen.

That our daughters may be as pillars, sculptured in palace style.
PSALM 144:12 NKJV

SONS

Father God, thank You for my son. When I consider the responsibilities of manhood that are in his future, I know I have a lot to teach him. There are some aspects of boyhood and adolescence that I only understand from study and observation. On the other hand, there are things I can teach him from a woman's perspective that will make him a better husband and father. So bring to my mind those things I need to discuss with him; give me discernment so I can address any issues with which he is struggling. Bless our relationship so it will enrich both our lives. Amen.

That our sons may be as plants grown up in their youth.
PSALM 144:12 NKJV

Dear God, I ask You to watch over my children. I don't know why I feel fearful for them today. I know You love them even more than I do, and You've seen every part of their lives from the moment they were conceived. Keep them in Your care today. If they're in physical danger just now, protect them. If they're facing ridicule or embarrassment today, remind them that You think they're awesome. If they're feeling discouragement or defeat at this moment, bring someone along to show them Your love. I thank You for hearing my prayer and knowing my heart. Amen.

The angel of the Lord encamps all around those who fear Him, and delivers them.
PSALM 34:7 NKJV

TIME FOR DISCUSSION

Lord, I need to have some talks with my teens. There are so many issues that crop up in this season of life. And right now, I feel swamped with my own concerns. But their maturing process won't wait until I have my life figured out. This is happening in real time. Show me the right time and place to have these important discussions. I don't want our talks to be awkward or cheesy. I want to be there for my children and come alongside them in the important things. Please guide me. In Jesus' name, amen.

*Bring them up in the training
and instruction of the Lord.*
EPHESIANS 6:4 NIV

SCHOOL DAYS

Father, my firstborn is starting school today. I'm proud and sad at the same time. This is another step toward my child's independence, and I'm not sure I'm ready for it. I'm thrilled at the progress she's made, but it also means she doesn't need me like she did before. Help her teacher, Lord, to be a good influence on my little girl. Let her instructor be kind and controlled, and never harsh in manner. Be with my child as she leaves my sight and care. Guard her body and mind, I pray. And help me let go in this small way. Amen.

*He has made everything
beautiful in its time.*
ECCLESIASTES 3:11 NIV

IT'S EMPTY

Heavenly Father, the last one is gone. And does it feel strange! All those years that I wanted peace and quiet—not true. What I wouldn't give now for a little noise! And all those times I felt like a short-order cook, chauffeur, tutor, and maid? Well, I don't know what to do with myself now that I only have to care for my husband and myself. Lord, I know it's Your plan that children grow up and leave home to enter the future You have for them. I need Your grace to accept this new season and learn to embrace its gifts. Amen.

Behold, children are a heritage from the LORD.
PSALM 127:3 NKJV

Confidantes and Mentors

FRIENDS

A friend loves at all times.

PROVERBS 17:17 NKJV

HOSPITALITY

Dear Lord, I need to improve my skills in hospitality. Because You have blessed me, I need to share with others. In fact, hospitality is one of those virtues the apostle Paul commanded of the church. Sharing my home with others is my Christian duty and also a great way to reach out to unbelievers whom I have befriended. Please let me not dread hosting others but rather find ways to make it doable and enjoyable for all. In Jesus' name, amen.

Use hospitality one to another without grudging.
1 PETER 4:9 KJV

THE REAL ME

Heavenly Father, so many people in my world wear masks. We earth dwellers are afraid to be real with others; we fear losing the respect and esteem of our peers. And, oddly enough, we're often afraid to be real with even You—and You know everything about us anyway. I want to be genuine in my approach and interaction with others, including You. Give me the courage to reject the lure of artificial "perfectness" and instead live out my life and relationships in a real way. Amen.

I have chosen the way of truth.
PSALM 119:30 NKJV

FRIENDS FOR EVERY NEED

Dear Heavenly Father, I am grateful for my friends. They are such a vital part of my life. When my family can't be there, my friends come through for me. When I need someone to gripe to, they will listen. When I need a kick to get me going again, they don't hesitate. My journey through life would be so lonely and unhappy without these amazing women who walk it with me. Thank You for blessing me through them. Help me return the favor. Amen.

A time to weep, and a time to laugh;
a time to mourn, and a time to dance.
ECCLESIASTES 3:4 NKJV

MOVING AND MAKING FRIENDS

God, I don't like change or new places.
I'd rather just stay in my comfort zone.
But that's not happening. Here I am in
a strange new environment. I miss my
old friends so much. I feel like crying just
thinking about them. But that won't do
any good, will it? I need some heavenly
moxie. It's time to square my shoulders,
walk in, smile, introduce myself, and
meet some new people. I guess I can
think of them as pre-friends. Help me not
to chicken out! Thank You. Amen.

*A man who has friends
must himself be friendly.*
PROVERBS 18:24 NKJV

RECONCILIATION

Dear Lord, I feel as if I'm on the set of *I Love Lucy* today, starring in an episode in which Ethel and Lucy have had a quarrel. I just can't believe that my friend and I had this disagreement. It feels so odd to have a chill between us instead of the warm camaraderie we've always shared. I confess I'm still hurt over what she said. Maybe she feels the same about the words that came out of my mouth. So please help us both to take the steps toward reconciliation. What do You want me to do right now to start repairing this friendship? Amen.

Be as ready to forgive others as God for Christ's sake has forgiven you.
EPHESIANS 4:32 PHILLIPS

FAITHFUL FRIENDSHIP

Father, I need to confront my friend. She seems to be making some bad decisions. I'm so afraid for her. Please keep me from joining in the discussions of others who are talking about her. Yet my just being silent isn't what she needs. I know some things about her life that have brought her to today; I know her secret pain and longings. Let me not betray her but rather come alongside to share the burden she's carrying and perhaps lovingly suggest another solution than the one she's trying. Heal her heart, Lord, and give me guidance in the process. In Christ's name, amen.

Faithful are the wounds of a friend.
PROVERBS 27:6 NKJV

MENTORING

Dear God, the Bible tells older women to mentor younger women. That's an element missing from my life. Although my mom did a great job of passing along the life lessons she'd learned, and we have a good relationship, I still need the insight and affirmation of an older woman. Lord, I need a trusted confidante, one who will help me succeed. I ask You to send someone like that my way in fulfillment of Your Word. And let me fill that role myself someday when I have the required résumé. Amen.

May [the aged women] teach the young women to be sober, to love their husbands, to love their children.
TITUS 2:4 KJV

A FRIEND IN NEED

O God, my friend was just diagnosed
with cancer. I'm shocked, devastated,
angry. I want to stay strong for her; but,
instead, I feel my own shaky emotions
every time I talk to her. I don't know Your
plan, but in my love for her, all I can ask
right now is that You heal her completely
and give me the courage to be strong for
her. Give us both Your peace, presence,
and comfort as we walk through the days
ahead. Let me be a true friend, now
more than ever. Amen.

A friend loves at all times.
PROVERBS 17:17 NKJV

THE BEAN THAT BLESSES

God, thank You for creating coffee beans. Coffee is one of life's basic pleasures. Our world sure depends on it to start the morning! And I really enjoy occasionally sipping a steaming latte. It's another one of those simple pleasures that I've taken for granted so many times. But I've heard about rationing in days past, and maybe there are some places still where coffee is hard to get. But I'm blessed today not only with a gourmet blend but a doughnut to go along with it. This is great! Thank You and amen.

Then God said, "I give you every seed-bearing plant on the face of the whole earth."
GENESIS 1:29 NIV

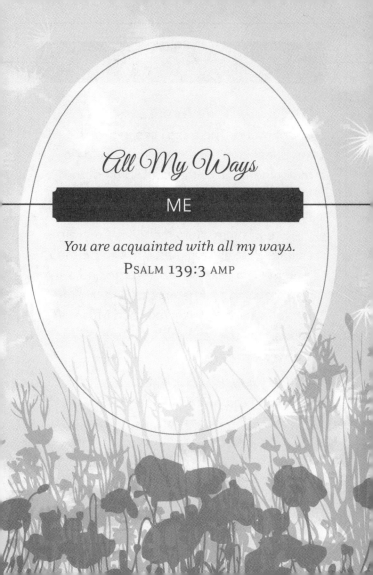

All My Ways

ME

You are acquainted with all my ways.

PSALM 139:3 AMP

THE SAME OLD ME

Lord, today I come to You a bit discouraged. The traits I see in myself are ones I don't like. It seems I could do much more for You without some of the inherent flaws of my personality. So help me overcome my defects or to use me in spite of them. Help me to love myself, as imperfect as I am, and strive to be the best me I can be. I know You can find a way around my impediments and use me for Your glory, just like You used Moses in spite of his speech problem. Amen.

You have searched me,
LORD, and you know me.
PSALM 139:1 NIV

NOT GOOD ENOUGH

Father, shopping for clothing at the mall makes me so insecure. The store windows are filled with posters of glamorous women in size zero clothing. I feel I will never "measure up" to these air-brushed supermodels. Like every other twenty-first century woman I know, I struggle with body image. Although these feelings of inferiority seem petty, and a bit self-centered, they are so real sometimes that I get depressed. I know that isn't what You want for me. Help me with these feelings and show me the way to triumph over them. In Christ's name, amen.

I praise you because I am fearfully and wonderfully made.
PSALM 139:14 NIV

TIMELY WISDOM

Lord, I wasted my time this afternoon watching a movie. I needed to do other things, but I got caught up in the plot. Now I'm running behind in my schedule. Thank You, Lord, for giving writers and moviemakers the gifts necessary to craft moving stories, sometimes life-changing dramas. But help me to use my time more wisely so I can enjoy this pleasure sans guilt. And, Lord, help me to guard my mind carefully when I'm selecting what to watch. Amen.

For the LORD gives wisdom;
from His mouth come
knowledge and understanding.
PROVERBS 2:6 NKJV

THE POWER OF WORDS

Father, my mouth sometimes gets me into trouble. Please keep me aware of the things I say that aren't right. Let me back up and apologize if I've hurt anyone. Better yet, let me consider my words before I cast them out on the wind. Once spoken, they can never be recalled. Your written Word is living, brilliant, and powerful; Jesus is the embodiment of it—the Living Word. My spoken earthly words are weighty as well; they can minister life or death to those who hear. I ask You to remind me of this throughout the day. Amen.

Death and life are in the power of the tongue: and they that love it shall eat the fruit thereof.
PROVERBS 18:21 KJV

NO SPIRIT OF FEAR

Father, I deal with a phobia. It isn't anything life threatening, but it's embarrassing. I haven't told anyone, and I'm hoping I never have to. But I ask You now to help me; I don't want my phobia to keep me from living the life You've planned for me. Help me to bring this fear to You; show me that You are in control, that You are the security system in my life. I ask this in Jesus' name, amen.

For God has not given us a spirit of fear, but a spirit of power and love and a sound mind.
2 TIMOTHY 1:7 PHILLIPS

FIXING MY THOUGHTS

God, today I'm having a pity party.
My thoughts are so focused on earthly
things that I am having trouble looking
up. I could mope around here all day,
but I guess it's time for the music to stop
and the party to end. Lord, You can't
work through me when I'm feeling sorry
for myself. Forgive me for my pettiness,
and let me respond to life with maturity.
Help me to focus on good, praiseworthy
things. In Christ's name, amen.

Fix your thoughts on what is
true, and honorable, and right,
and pure, and lovely, and admirable.
PHILIPPIANS 4:8 NLT

A MODEL OF MODESTY

Dear Father, there is a lot of talk in the Christian women's community about modesty. It's an issue that really goes counter to our culture. Fashion today is more about being "hot" than anything else. Clothing often seems to reveal more than it covers. Yet, God, I don't want the way I dress to send out a message that contradicts my relationship with You. Let me remember that attracting attention to my body puts the focus on me, not You. And that my dressing immodestly could be a source of struggle for my brothers in Christ. Modesty can be tasteful and beautiful; help me model it. Amen.

I desire therefore that. . .women adorn themselves in modest apparel. . . which is proper for women professing godliness, with good works.
1 TIMOTHY 2:8-10 NKJV

FADELESS BEAUTY

Dear God, I'm getting older. That's not news to You, I know. You've seen my journey from day one. But now my body is revolting and my hormones are rebelling. I don't like looking in the mirror because it shocks me to see lines on my face. Inside, I don't feel old; but my body doesn't agree. Still, Lord, help me remember that my identity in You is changeless and my beauty in You is fadeless. The magazines may say differently, but I know that in Your sight, I have a loveliness that time can't touch. Amen.

The unfading loveliness of a calm and gentle spirit, a thing very precious in the eyes of God.
1 PETER 3:4 PHILLIPS

FIRST GLIMPSE OF GRAY

Lord, I found a gray hair today. I guess I could call it silver (not good) or white (even worse). Whatever the tint is, it's not the color I was born with! I realize the aging process is part of the death process and death in our world is the result of sin. So I feel perfectly justified in not wanting to age. But I must acknowledge the fact that I cannot continually stay in the youthful season of life. Please give me whatever kind of grace I need to resist adopting a nasty attitude about growing older, and renew my strength every day. Amen.

The outward man does indeed suffer wear and tear, but every day the inward man receives fresh strength.
2 Corinthians 4:16 Phillips

FOOD BUDGETING

God, I'm really struggling today with self-worth because I just feel so fat. I know I need discipline—to eat less and exercise more. I do pretty well for a while, but then I get off track. And dieting feels like fake living. I mean, who seriously thinks non-fat cheese is delicious? I see skinny people every day who can wear stylish clothing and aren't afraid to stand in the front row when group pictures are taken. I want that kind of freedom, Lord, so help me "budget" my food so I can rid myself of feeling overblown. Amen.

But the fruit of the Spirit is. . .self-control.
GALATIANS 5:22–23 NIV

GOSSIP

Lord, I got caught in gossip today. I didn't mean to though. A group of us were just talking about this and that, and You know how women are. We're so into relationships and what others are doing. Before long, the conversation had dug itself a little too deep into someone else's life. I tried to stop listening but didn't try hard enough. By the time we broke up our little gabfest, I felt terribly guilty. Please forgive me, Father. Give me the courage to make the right decision next time; help me refuse to listen to negative stories about someone who is not there to defend him- or herself. In Jesus' name, amen.

Let all. . .evil speaking be put away from you, with all malice.
Ephesians 4:31 NKJV

MUSIC

Dear Lord, music is the universal language of the human family. Today, music is available on a multitude of electronic devices. And there are so many genres—an array of listening options. Some appeal to me; others don't. But I want to base my choices on Your principles. What I listen to will affect my mood, my attitude, and my spiritual state of being. Holy Spirit, give me discernment. Let the music to which I listen not go counter to what You're trying to do in me. Amen.

*Whatsoever ye do,
do all to the glory of God.*
1 CORINTHIANS 10:31 KJV

ADMIRATION

Dear Father, I want to be admired. You made women to be beautiful, and You designed men to appreciate that fact. But there is an appropriate time and place for such admiration. Please help me avoid the temptation to attract attention in ways that aren't right. This deep hunger to be beautiful in a man's eyes is so strong. I ask You to help me resist temptation and to dress and act in such a way that I'll have no regrets. Amen.

For no one ever hated his own flesh, but nourishes and cherishes it, just as the Lord does the church.
Ephesians 5:29 NKJV

COVETING

God, it's so easy to break the tenth commandment: Do not covet (see Exodus 20:17). Coveting is a way of life for many in our world. But You say we shouldn't compare ourselves with the "Joneses," nor envy them and what they have. Whatever You've given me is to be enjoyed and received, not held up for inspection. Teach me a deeper gratefulness for Your blessings. In Jesus' name, amen.

*Let your conduct be
without covetousness.*
HEBREWS 13:5 NKJV

GOLDEN WORDS NEEDED

Heavenly Father, today I need affirming words. You know that words are important to me as a woman. You also know that I struggle with self-worth. The other people in my world don't always meet my need to be affirmed verbally, and I can't expect them to fulfill every void in my life. So, Lord, let me look to and in Your Word to find the love and encouragement I need. In Jesus' name, amen.

A word fitly spoken is like apples of gold in settings of silver.
PROVERBS 25:11 NKJV

POISE

Heavenly Father, I need poise—that kind of gracious manner and behavior that characterized women of past generations. It seems to be disdained in my culture. Women now are expected and encouraged to be free spirits—unrestricted by convention and decorum. But I cringe when I observe women using crude language, slouching in their seats, and adopting careless ways of walking and eating. I don't want to seem prissy and uppity, but I do want to guard against being too informal. Help me develop the traits that portray womanhood as the gentle, beautiful, fascinating gender You designed. Amen.

Like a gold ring in a pig's snout is a beautiful woman who shows no discretion.
PROVERBS 11:22 NIV

A CRAVING FOR ROMANCE

Romance is something I long for, Father God. The woman's heart You gave me delights in the theme of romance— strong hero, lovely maiden, fierce obstacles, and final relationship. You understand how deeply I yearn to be loved and delighted in. And no man on earth can totally meet this need; I know that. But there is a hunger inside that awakens more fully when I read a novel or watch a movie. Let me remember that, though my earthly female desires will always be part of my world, only You can fill the craving for an eternal and completely dependable love. Amen.

"I will betroth you to me forever."
HOSEA 2:19 NIV

On the Journey

SPIRITUAL LESSONS/ MILESTONES

I feel sure that the one who has begun his good work in you will go on developing it until the day of Jesus Christ.

PHILIPPIANS 1:6 PHILLIPS

LESSONS IN TRUST

Heavenly Father, teach me to trust. I know it's an area of weakness for me. In spite of the fact that I know Your character and Your track record, I find it so difficult to relinquish to You the important areas of life. Oh, I say that I will, and I do put forth effort to rely on You, but we both know that, in my heart, I find it hard to let You handle everything. So take my hand, Lord, and teach me to trust. You're the Master; I am forever Your student. In Christ's name, amen.

I have put my trust in the Lord God, that I may declare all Your works.
PSALM 73:28 NKJV

DIVINE GUIDANCE

Dear Lord, it's so hard sometimes to know what Your will is. You don't write specific instructions in the sky nor emblazon them on a marquee. So how can I know exactly what You want me to do? How can I keep from making a big mistake? How can I proceed with this decision? I ask today that You would give me wisdom, send me guidance as I seek Your will. Through a person, a thought, a scripture, let me sense Your leading for this situation. I want my life to honor Your plan for me. In Christ's name, amen.

If any of you lacks wisdom, you should ask God, who gives generously to all without finding fault, and it will be given to you.
JAMES 1:5 NIV

RESTORED

God, I'm grappling with failure. In something in which I wanted so badly to succeed, I've had a less than stellar performance. In fact, humiliating is more like it. I've failed to accomplish my own goals. And I've disappointed others I care about. So where do I go from here? I'm not a quitter, yet I admit I'm lacking motivation to try again. Please give me the courage I need, and help me remember all those Bible characters who refused to be defined by failure, but instead sought grace, attempted the challenge again, and triumphed. Let my story be like theirs, I pray. In Jesus' name, amen.

Restore to me the joy of Your salvation, and uphold me by Your generous Spirit.
PSALM 51:12 NKJV

DEEP SURRENDER

Lord, I need to surrender to You. You've shown me an area of my life that I've been trying to rule. I know You need the keys to every room in my heart, and so here I am, bringing this one to You. Surrender means I give You permission to change, clean out, and add things. Waving the white flag isn't really easy, but it's the way to true joy. Thank You for showing me that. Amen.

But now, O Lord, You are our Father; we are the clay, and You our potter; and all we are the work of Your hand.
ISAIAH 64:8 NKJV

TO-DO LISTS

God, I like to know what's coming up next in my life. I like to chart the items requiring some kind of action from me. To-do lists are my way of planning out the day and week. The lists keep me on track, but anything can be detrimental if it becomes too important. Help me not to plot and plan my life so completely that there is no room for divine interruptions, for Providence to intervene. Give me patience with those who cause my day to go awry; let me see beyond the irritation to what You have in mind. In Jesus' name, amen.

*We can make our plans, but the
LORD determines our steps.*
PROVERBS 16:9 NLT

ENDURANCE REQUIRED

I'm finding, Lord, that the Christian life is one that requires endurance. It isn't enough to start well. So let me patiently and steadily move down the road to Christlikeness. I know difficulties will come; I've faced some already. It reminds me of the words of the second verse of "Amazing Grace": "Through many dangers, toils, and snares, I have already come. 'Tis grace that brought me safe thus far, and grace will lead me home." In Your name, amen.

Let us run with endurance the race that is set before us.
HEBREWS 12:1 NKJV

A GOD OF PROCESS

Dear Lord, so many things are instantaneous in my world. From fast food to instant credit, we can satisfy our penchant for immediate gratification at every juncture. But I have to keep reminding myself that You often work by process. When it comes to the work You're doing in me, You use the steady maturing of Your Word within me to make me more like Jesus. You, the Master Gardener, water the seeds, prune the unnecessary limbs, and watch over me carefully as the fruit of my life continues to ripen. Instead of being impatient, I aim to revel in Your timely and tender loving care. Amen.

But grow in grace, and in the knowledge of our Lord and Saviour Jesus Christ.
2 PETER 3:18 KJV

EVEN MORE SURRENDER

O Lord, I thought I had surrendered my will to You. But today I've discovered that there's another area I need to relinquish to Your control. This surrender thing isn't easy; in fact, it's hard. Painful even. It takes determination and guts. Like Abraham laying his promised son on the altar, let me spread before You my cherished possession that is threatening Your place in my life. Let me keep You first in my love. You've promised to provide a ram. So I surrender. In Jesus' name, amen.

I once thought these things were valuable, but now I consider them worthless because of what Christ has done.
PHILIPPIANS 3:7 NLT

CRITICISM AND JUDGING

Dear Lord, criticism can be so hurtful. It's easy to give, but so difficult to receive. Sometimes people paraphrase Matthew 7:1 as "Don't judge." But it actually means "Don't judge unless you want to be judged." I don't think we realize that when we criticize others, we open ourselves up to the same kind of scrutiny. I'm not very good at living up to this standard. Help me to be less critical of others. Check me, Holy Spirit, when I start to say something judgmental. Amen.

Set a guard over my mouth, LORD;
keep watch over the door of my lips.
PSALM 141:3 NIV

Bitterness is like cancer, God. It grows and takes over, squeezing out life. I don't want to be marked or consumed by bitterness. Let me not hold to the injustices I've experienced. Help me accept Your healing touch and let go of the beginnings of bitterness in my soul. As Joseph noted in the Old Testament, You can turn things meant for evil into good. Please do that in my life. In Christ's name, amen.

Let all bitterness, wrath, anger, clamor, and evil speaking be put away from you, with all malice.
EPHESIANS 4:31 NKJV

GRANTING FORGIVENESS

Heavenly Father, I need to forgive someone who wronged me. I know it's the right thing, but it's so difficult. I can't do it in my own strength. Give me the power to extend grace to this person. Put Your love in my heart so I can have a gracious attitude and heart of mercy. The Bible tells me to forgive because I have been forgiven. This is my chance to put it into practice. I'm leaning on Your power. In Jesus' name, amen.

"And whenever you stand praying, if you have anything against anyone, forgive him, that your Father in heaven may also forgive you your trespasses."
MARK 11:25 NKJV

DELICATE, POWERFUL FAITH

God, faith is such a delicate concept, yet so mighty in its power. Faith isn't something I can wrap my arms around, but it is something I can rest my soul in. Hebrews 11:1 says it's "the evidence of things not seen." That means it's like a virtual item—something that already exists, though you can't hold it in your hand. Faith is sometimes trivialized in our world, but it is of utmost importance to You. Please increase my faith, O Lord. In Christ's name, amen.

Now faith is the substance of things hoped for, the evidence of things not seen.
HEBREWS 11:1 KJV

TRADITIONAL VALUES

Father God, what are traditional values? So many people speak of them today in political and religious circles. In America, we usually mean lifestyle principles built on the Judeo-Christian understanding of scripture. But, what about traditional values for the Muslim world? The Hindu culture? The Buddhist way of life? The meaning of *traditional* is defined by the tradition one embraces. Lord, I thank You that I am not dependent on American history for my values. While I love my country and am proud of our national heritage, I can claim the precepts for living found in Your Word whatever my ethnicity, residence, or background. Amen.

Your statutes are always righteous;
give me understanding that I may live.
PSALM 119:144 NIV

Humanness and Hormones

EMOTIONS

For he knows how we are formed,
he remembers that we are dust.

PSALM 103:14 NIV

HORMONAL HAVOC

I'm having a hard time today, God. My hormones are really out of whack. Every little thing seems monstrous. I don't want to nurture anyone, cook meals, stay at work, or even be nice! What I really want to do is get in my pajamas, cuddle up with a quilt, and be alone. But I know I have responsibilities. And You have blessed me with a family, a job, and a life. Help me hold it together, Lord. Or, even better, please hold it together for me. And remind me to pause before I speak today—then maybe I'll have less apologies to make tomorrow.

We are. . .never abandoned by God. We get knocked down, but we are not destroyed.
2 CORINTHIANS 4:9 NLT

Dear God, please help me hold together the pieces of my life. My to-do list seems endless. There is always someone needing me. There are constant demands on my energy and sanity. I feel like I go through life in a state of exhaustion. I know that keeps me from being at my peak. And I know You want me to care for my health. But I'm stuck in a cycle of busyness that has no end in sight. Show me what I can change, Lord. Show me how to get the emotional and physical wellness I need. Amen.

He gives power to the weak, and to those who have no might He increases strength.... Those who wait on the LORD shall renew their strength; they shall mount up with wings like eagles, they shall run and not be weary, they shall walk and not faint.
ISAIAH 40:29, 31 NKJV

BUOYANCY OF FAITH

God, I've seen swollen rivers; I've watched raging water destroy entire communities. And right now, I feel like the tide of my life is reaching flood level. I'm struggling to keep my head above water, but the waves keep crashing over me. This struggle with depression is almost more than I can bear. Sometimes I just want to surrender to the current and slip under the water. But others are depending on me and You would be hurt if I chose to end this journey that way. Please hold me up in this flood; Your hands are the only ones that can. Amen.

"When you pass through the waters, I will be with you; and through the rivers, they shall not overflow you."
ISAIAH 43:2 NKJV

TEARS

I've heard, God, that tears speak their own language. If that's true, then You made women verbal in two ways—words and tears. Being the gentler, more emotional reflection of Your image, we tend to cry easily. Like most women, I cry for a variety of reasons, and sometimes for no reason at all, like today. But since You read what's in my heart, I know You understand. Thank You for valuing my tears. Amen.

Put my tears into Your bottle;
are they not in Your book?
PSALM 56:8 NKJV

MOMENT BY MOMENT

Father in Heaven, I have a tendency to try to live a week or month at a time. It's difficult for me to limit myself to one day, one hour, one minute. But that's how You want me to live. You know that projecting into the future causes me to wonder and worry about things that haven't happened yet. You also know that I can't be any good to anyone if my head is in the clouds, thinking about the future. So help me live in today—it's all I have at the moment. Amen.

"Does He not see my ways, and count all my steps?"
JOB 31:4 NKJV

ANGER

God, I need a solution for my anger. Sometimes I let it take over then end up regretting what it leads me to say or do. As I pray and study and grow closer to You, show me ways to control it. Guide me to the right verses to memorize and incorporate into my life. Lead me to someone who can keep me accountable. And, most of all, help me strive for self-control. Amen.

If it is possible, as much as depends on you, live peaceably with all men. Beloved, do not avenge yourselves, but rather give place to wrath; for it is written, "Vengeance is Mine, I will repay," says the Lord.
ROMANS 12:18–19 NKJV

REAL PEACE

Father, peace is an elusive emotion. So many people talk about peace, but few can claim it. You promised to give us Your peace, a calm assurance that You are present and sovereign in all our ways. I want more of this peace every day. Although there are many upsetting things in my world, Your peace will help me cope with them all. Amid Your peace, I am neither troubled nor afraid, merely allowing myself to bask in Your presence. Amen.

"Peace I leave with you,
My peace I give to you."
JOHN 14:27 NKJV

DE-STRESS

Lord, because it has become so overused, the word *stress* hardly affects us. Of course, we know the effects of stress never fade, but often, the punch of the word itself does. Still, I'm facing stress today; help me deal with it appropriately. Let me not take it out on my family or dump it on my coworkers. Help me remember to take it to You and leave it there in exchange for Your peace and strength. Amen.

Praise be to the Lord, to God our Savior,
who daily bears our burdens.
PSALM 68:19 NIV

NEVER REALLY ALONE

Heavenly Father, I'm lonely today. There is no one with whom I can share what is going on in my life right now. Oh, I have friends, but no one who would really understand this. But You created me, and You know me like no one else. I ask You today to let me feel Your presence with me. It's a terrible thing to be alone, but You promised You'd never leave. So, I know You are with me. I'm grateful for Your constant love and care. In Jesus' name, amen.

God has said: "I will never leave you nor forsake you."
HEBREWS 13:5 PHILLIPS

IT'S ALL GOOD

Lord, it feels good to be alive! When I got out of bed this morning, I had this wonderful sense of well-being. Some days I awaken with something negative on my mind, some trouble on the horizon, or some ache in my body. But today I feel great in mind, spirit, and body. This road of life has both mountains and valleys. But right now, I'm going to enjoy the mountain— the brightness, the beauty, and the refreshing that will help me face any challenge that comes my way today or tomorrow. I love You, Lord. Thank You for good surprises! In Jesus' name, amen.

Oh, give thanks to the LORD, for He is good! For His mercy endures forever.
PSALM 107:1 NKJV

MY REFUGE

Dear God, I bring You my fears today. I ask You to settle my qualms and give me assurance that You are present with me. Knowing that, I can face anything. Like the disciples in the boat with You during the storm, I don't need to let my fears shake me; You are onboard and even nature obeys Your voice. Thank You for being my strength and my refuge. Amen.

I will say of the LORD, He is my refuge and my fortress: my God; in him will I trust.
PSALM 91:2 KJV

SLOTHFULNESS

Father God, I've put myself in a bind because I procrastinated. I knew this was looming ahead of me, but I wanted to do other things first. Or, at least, I wanted to leave the task until the right time. But now, there is no more time, and I'm not prepared. Please help me, Lord, working all things to my good. Amen.

Make the most of every opportunity.
EPHESIANS 5:16 NLT

FILLED WITH PRAISE

Father, complaining is on Your list of dislikes. When the ancient Israelites griped in the desert, they were awarded another forty years of wandering. I don't want to be like them. When I'm tempted to complain, remind me of their story. It would be easy to moan and groan today, but You don't ask us to do what is easy. You ask us to do only what is right. So help me focus on praise just now. Amen.

Let my mouth be filled with Your praise and with Your glory all the day.
PSALM 71:8 NKJV

The Small Stuff

TRIVIA

"Who dares despise the day of small things?"

ZECHARIAH 4:10 NIV

CALM AMID THE STORM

Lord, I'm running late today! Before I even got out of bed, the day seemed to go haywire! I overslept, had to skip breakfast, had a horrible commute, forgot to thaw the entrée for tonight's dinner, and had a few tense words with my family. So I feel really out of sorts and have this premonition that I'm going to be playing catch-up all day long. Help me to focus on You on this ill-fitting day, and let my attitude not match it! Amen.

"You will keep him in perfect peace, whose mind is stayed on You."
Isaiah 26:3 nkjv

Moving is highly overrated, God. Oh, how I hate the disarray of boxes and the jumbled schedule involved! Moving means so many details to oversee—address change, new bank accounts and driver's license, new doctors and dentists, new stores, new driving routine, and on and on. Help me, Lord, to adjust as smoothly as possible. And thank You, that no matter where I unpack my boxes, You're already there. Amen.

If I rise on the wings of the dawn,
if I settle on the far side of the sea,
even there your hand will guide me,
your right hand will hold me fast.
PSALM 139:9-10 NIV

WASHED CLEAN

Laundry is the bane of my life, Lord. I don't enjoy the sorting and folding. The washing and drying aren't that bad, but of course, machines do that for me! Still, laundry day reminds me that nothing good comes without work. To have fresh clothing in the closet, I have to labor. Of course, with salvation, I didn't have to do the work. But Someone else did. The price Your Son paid was much greater than a little bit of time. And all I have to do is accept Him. How cut-and-dried is that! Amen.

Christ loved the church and gave himself up for her to make her holy, cleansing her by the washing with water through the word.
EPHESIANS 5:25-26 NIV

REST FOR A WHILE

It's vacation time, God, and am I ever ready! There's nothing like a few days of relaxation! I'm glad You built the concept of rest into the structure of our world. On the seventh day of creation, You rested. And You even designed laws for the Old Testament Hebrews so they would have to rest. (You knew those workaholics would ignore the Sabbath if the consequences weren't serious!) And now, I have the chance to take some time off for rest. Because of You, I am going to enjoy it to the fullest! Amen.

"Now come along to some quiet place by yourselves, and rest for a little while."
MARK 6:31 PHILLIPS

PERSPECTIVE ON CLEANING

Well, Lord, here I am cleaning toilets!
This is definitely not my favorite
household task; I much more prefer the
tidy and glamorous aspects of home
maintenance. But, like so many parts of
life, cleaning toilets is necessary. So while
I'm scrubbing and shining, help me see
it as a service. When I perform my daily
duties with a glad heart, I am honoring
You. And I'm also ministering to the
family You've given me. Thank You,
Lord, for indoor plumbing and for a new
perspective. Amen.

*And whatever you do,
whether in word or deed, do it
all in the name of the Lord Jesus.*
COLOSSIANS 3:17 NIV

TRAVEL PRAYER

Dear Lord, my travel plans are complete. In just a few hours, I will be on my way. Please go with me as I travel; grant me safety, and let my life be a witness of You to my fellow travelers. Please go before me to my destination; bless those with whom I will interact and who will provide for my needs during this time. Thank You for modern modes of transportation; how grateful I am that my conveyance isn't a wagon, buggy, or coach. May this trip refresh me, and may I draw closer to You while I'm away from home. Amen.

*Let the words of my mouth,
and the meditation of my heart,
be acceptable in thy sight, O Lord,
my strength, and my redeemer.*
PSALM 19:14 KJV

STUCK ON THE HIGHWAY!

Father God, I'm stuck in traffic! I am going to be late. This is so frustrating! I even left a few minutes early, but it hasn't done me any good! I've already been sitting here for untold minutes. Oh, I should be calm and unruffled, but I feel irritated and hyper. I know You don't intervene in every instance of our lives; there are some parts of life that are just imperfect. So I'm not asking You to miraculously clear the highway lanes, but I'm requesting the grace to accept this, the tranquillity of spirit needed to adjust my day, and the joy of knowing You're stuck here with me. In Christ's name, amen.

The joy of the LORD is your strength.
NEHEMIAH 8:10 KJV

COMPUTER CRASH

I can't believe it, Lord! Although it was fine yesterday, today my computer crashed. Hard drive totally zapped. I know it's not as high on the disaster scale as many global events today, but to me, it's pretty awful. It's inconvenient and frustrating—there were family records, pictures, and documents on there that we need. Lord, would You work a miracle and breath new life into the motherboard of my desktop? If not, please give me the peace to accept things as they are, the energy to start over again, and the wisdom to use an external hard drive in the future.

Be pleased to save me, LORD;
come quickly, LORD, to help me.
PSALM 40:13 NIV

SHOES!

Dear Lord, thank You for shoes to match my mood. There are heels for glamorous events, flats for casual days, athletic shoes for exercise and outdoor play, boots for rain and cold, and slippers for shuffling around my kitchen in the early morning. But the most important footwear is mentioned in the list of biblical armor. No matter what I wear on my physical feet, help me remember to grab my spiritual shoes before I head out the door. In Christ's name, amen.

With your feet fitted with the readiness that comes from the gospel of peace.
EPHESIANS 6:15 NIV

A Broken World

GRIEF/LOSS

*Surely He has borne our griefs
and carried our sorrows.*

Isaiah 53:4 NKJV

LITTLE ONES

Father, my friend had a miscarriage. I know many women have miscarriages every day. But, God, surely every one of these tiny humans are seen and grieved by You. I don't understand why this happened, but I know our world is so broken. The death of this precious little one reminds me that heaven is our real home; someday You will replace our sorrows with eternal happiness. But for now, Lord, surround my friend with Your strength and comfort; give her the assurance that You are keeping her little baby safe until she arrives. Amen.

"Do not be afraid, for I am with you;
I will bring your children from the
east and gather you from the west."
ISAIAH 43:5 NIV

THE TWIST IN NATURE

God, there was a horrific natural disaster today. The images on the TV screen tore at my heart. Homes were destroyed, communities devastated, and human lives lost. This world we love can sometimes turn on us and cause terrible pain. There are those who blame You; but they're wrong. You planned perfection, but we messed it up by allowing sin to enter our planet. Thank You for the promise that, someday, there will be a new earth. Meanwhile, please minister to the victims of this tragedy right now. In Christ's name, amen.

It is plain to anyone with eyes to see that at the present time all created life groans in a sort of universal travail.
ROMANS 8:22 PHILLIPS

TERROR AND VIOLENCE

Dear Father, the news media has reported another large-scale terror incident. These kinds of things are so frightening to me. I can't imagine what it's like for those directly involved. Please be with the families of those who were killed; give leaders wisdom as they deal with the threats we face because of hatred and violence. I know, Lord, that peace will not reign on our earth until You set up Your kingdom. So until that day let me be an instrument of Your peace to those I meet. In Christ's name, amen.

For You have been a shelter for me,
a strong tower from the enemy.
PSALM 61:3 NKJV

SHARED COMFORT

My friend lost a family member this week, God. I don't know what to say. I've been trying to work out the right words, but every one of them seems superficial and unfeeling to my ears. I don't want to be insensitive, but neither do I want to be melodramatic. Please, Father, guide my words; speak comfort through my lips today. Like those who have come alongside me in my dark hours, let me minister to my hurting friend today. Amen.

For he gives us comfort in our trials so that we in turn may be able to give the same sort of strong sympathy to others in theirs.
2 CORINTHIANS 1:4 PHILLIPS

HOMELESS

Father, today I was approached by a homeless person and, mentally, I recoiled. I admit that I struggle with uncertainty in this kind of situation. I've heard stories about supposedly homeless people who either just don't want to work or are too incapacitated to hold down a job. Yet I'm conflicted when I recall Your words that when we care for those who are naked, cold, and hungry, we are actually serving You. Give me discernment, Lord. I can't minister in every type of environment, but if there is someone I need to touch, please prompt me. In Jesus' name, amen.

"I was hungry and you gave Me food;
I was thirsty and you gave Me drink;
I was a stranger and you took Me in."
MATTHEW 25:35 NKJV

LITTLE CHILDREN

Father God, there are so many hurting children in the world. I've seen their pictures—the missing ones on the milk cartons and the starving ones in the relief organizations' advertising. I don't know why so many children are mistreated, abused, and killed, nor why thousands work like adults to support their family then go to bed hungry. But I do know that, although children are very special to You, You don't interfere with our free choice, even if it causes pain for someone else. So tonight please comfort every little child who is frightened and hurting. In Your name, amen.

"Whoever receives one little child like this in My name receives Me."
MATTHEW 18:5 NKJV

NO MORE STING

Father God, I'm attending a funeral today. And I remember again why death is our enemy. It robs us of loved ones; it severs our relationships; it causes us pain. I want to be strong, but I know that when death visits my family, I forget all about the grief process and working through the hurt. I just feel empty; my world is tilted and unnatural. Yet I hold on to the promise that You conquered death, knowing that one day, this enemy of all humanity won't have power over us anymore. Until then, please comfort me and others as we grieve. Amen.

"Where, O death, is your victory?
Where, O death, is your sting?"
1 CORINTHIANS 15:55 NIV

GOD'S KNITTING

Dear Heavenly Father, today I'm grieving the tragedy of abortion. Every woman has been touched by this crisis in one way or another. Abortion isn't just a procedure that stops a pregnancy; it's a dramatic moment that changes lives forever. Right now, Lord, I pray for all who have been hurt by abortion—the mothers, the fathers, the doctors, the medical staff, the lawmakers. Minister healing and redemption to broken lives. Help us protect and cherish these precious not-yet-born human beings. In Jesus' name, amen.

For you created my inmost being; you knit me together in my mother's womb.
PSALM 139:13 NIV

THE ASHES OF DIVORCE

Divorce has invaded my family, dear God. I want to reach out to the couple involved, but some things can only be worked out by the husband and wife. This may be awkward and painful for all of us. Help me love them; let our family minister without condemning. Please show mercy and bring this pair to a point of reconciliation. The Bible says You hate divorce because You know the pain it brings to everyone. But it also says that You can bring beauty from ashes. I ask You to do that for this couple. In Christ's name, amen.

Beauty for ashes, the oil of joy for mourning, the garment of praise for the spirit of heaviness.
Isaiah 61:3 KJV

HURTING CHILDREN

Heavenly Father, the news reports of child abuse are sickening. Some little children are treated so terribly by adults—sometimes even by their own parents—who are many times their size. I know that it's often the result of frustration spun out of control. But other times it's pure vicious intent. My heart hurts for every little boy or girl who has to endure that kind of pain. Please be with the hurting children tonight, Lord. Hold them close, and ease their pain. In Christ's name, amen.

"You must let little children come to me, and you must never stop them. The kingdom of Heaven belongs to little children like these!"
MATTHEW 19:14 PHILLIPS

DINING LUXURY

Dear God, it's a blessing to eat out! I love the luxury of sitting at a table, being served food cooked by someone else. I know this privilege can be abused; it's probably not good stewardship to eat more in a restaurant than at home, but used correctly, how awesome it is! Thank You for providing me the resources to dine out. Help me to be a good customer, and let me make You look good by treating the server with kindness and leaving a good tip. Amen!

He. . .gave us rain from heaven, and fruitful seasons, filling our hearts with food and gladness.
ACTS 14:17 KJV

All Things Bright and Beautiful

NATURE

All things bright and beautiful,
All creatures great and small,
All things wise and wonderful:
The Lord God made them all.
CECIL F. ALEXANDER,
"ALL THINGS BRIGHT AND BEAUTIFUL"

SNOW LIKE WOOL

Lord, I love the snow. I'm watching the snowflakes flutter past my window and frost the winter landscape with white. There is something so magical and mesmerizing about falling snow. And You are the Creator of this beauty. Your fingerprint is on every crystal that falls to the earth—each unique in design, a testament to Your greatness in things both big and small. Thank You for thinking of snow—it makes my heart happy. Amen.

He gives snow like wool;
He scatters the frost like ashes.
PSALM 147:16 NKJV

SPLENDOROUS TREES

Heavenly Father, what a wonder are trees! So much more than branches to climb, shade to enjoy, and logs to burn—trees are majestic tributes to Your splendor. People living in deserts and prairies know the difference trees make in the landscape; they add beauty and protection. But, in addition to their aesthetic value, trees convey deep truths. They display what a Christian should be like—rooted deep, connected to a Source, full of life, bearing fruit, and standing strong in the storm. Lord, help me be like a tree. In Jesus' name, amen.

*And he shall be like a tree
planted by the rivers of water.*
PSALM 1:3 KJV

HARVEST COLORS

Dear God, the fall foliage is gorgeous! It reminds me of those kaleidoscopes I used to look in when I was a child—a shifting, sparkling mix of color. I know that autumn is the time of year when things begin to die, but how beautifully You frame their demise. Pumpkins and gourds, brilliant leaves in saffron and crimson, plump chrysanthemums—a glorious treat for the senses. Thank You, God, for giving us some dazzle in which to bid summer farewell. How great You are! Amen.

"While the earth remains, seedtime and harvest, cold and heat, winter and summer, and day and night shall not cease."
GENESIS 8:22 NKJV

TRIUMPHANT DAY

Lord, is any day more glorious than Easter morning? Thank You for triumphing over death for me! Because You live, I shall live forever, too! And today, the earth celebrates Your victory. The world is dressed in spring finery—tulips beaming, trees budding, grass sprouting, and birds chirping. There is energy and life in the very breeze that blows outside. All of creation has heard Your voice and awakened from winter slumber. I join in their chorus—You are the Creator of all things living, and worthy to be praised. Amen.

The flowers appear on the earth; the time of the singing of birds is come.
SONG OF SOLOMON 2:12 KJV

CONSIDERING FLOWERS

Creator God, I am always amazed by the things You've made. The flowers blooming outside this summer are so delicate, yet so durable. From tiny seeds or bulbs they push forth toward the sun, breaking through the soil and raising up in fragile beauty. Petals soft as velvet and deep in color, the flowers add grace to the countryside. Yet they are incredibly strong. With the sun and rain You provide, they remain all season, delighting our eyes and hearts. Thank You for blessing us with their beauty and using them as a reminder that we need not worry. Amen.

And why take ye thought for raiment? Consider the lilies of the field.
MATTHEW 6:28 KJV

THE SEA

Father, I stand beside the ocean and gaze in wonder once again. What a vast expanse it is! The Bible tells us You formed the seas on the third day of Creation. It must have been an incredible sight—the waters being gathered together. And the seashore is one of my favorite places. I love to walk along the beach, scooping damp sand with my toes, hearing the cry of the gulls, and tasting the salty breeze. Thank You, Lord, for sharing Your sea with me. I feel close to You in this vastness. Amen.

The sea is his, and he made it.
PSALM 95:5 KJV

RUGGED MOUNTAINS, GREAT GOD

O God, when I look at the rugged mountains, I realize again how great You are. Guardians of the earth, stretching toward the heavens, they bear magnificent witness to Your power. In our Christian walk, Lord, we use mountains to symbolize great victories or celebrations. And Your Word tells us that our faith, be it as small as a mustard seed, can move mountains. What power we can garnish with You in our lives! Today, Lord, my eyes are fixed on You as I stand in awe of Your handiwork and revel in the power of a mountain-moving faith. Amen.

Before the mountains were brought forth, or ever You had formed the earth and the world, even from everlasting to everlasting, You are God.

PSALM 90:2 NKJV

COMMON SPARROWS

Out there on the grass, searching for food on this winter day, are common sparrows. This scene reminds me of a scripture verse in which You say that, although You do care about one little sparrow, You care much more about me. And that I should never be afraid, for I am worth much more to You than many sparrows. I revel in the fact that I am precious in Your sight! I don't have to strive for Your attention, for I am important in Your eyes! Thank You for reminding me today that I'm valued and loved. Amen.

"Not a single sparrow falls to the ground without your Father's knowledge.... Never be afraid, then—you are far more valuable than sparrows."
MATTHEW 10:29, 31 PHILLIPS

UNMARKED GIFTS

Father God, thank You for the gifts You send in unmarked packages. Sometimes we don't recognize them at first, but they prove to be immeasurable in worth. Those with special needs are gifts that require extra care, but who give back to us in ways we'd never imagine. I wish there were no disabilities, but our world is imperfect, and that includes the genetic code. Yet You wrap the most amazing people in these unexpected ways and then step back to see if we'll discover them. Help me, Lord, always to do that. Amen.

"But each one has his own gift from God, one in this manner and another in that."
1 CORINTHIANS 7:7 NKJV

All Now Mysterious

QUESTIONS/TRIALS

"Be still, my soul: thy God doth undertake to guide the future, as He has the past. Thy hope, thy confidence let nothing shake; all now mysterious shall be bright at last."

KATHARINA A. VON SCHLEGEL,
"BE STILL, MY SOUL"

UNEXPECTED ROUTE

Heavenly Father, I'm struggling with this circumstance in my life. I thought I understood Your plan for me, and this doesn't seem to fit. Maybe this is the result of an unwise decision I've made. Then again, perhaps this is one of those paths You allow that make no sense at the time but serve a higher purpose in Your plan to make me more like Jesus. Either way, God, please help me not to worry over things I can't change, and give me the grace I need to accept and adjust. Let me remember that Your Son also once walked a painful path.

But the path of the just is as the shining light, that shineth more and more unto the perfect day.
PROVERBS 4:18 KJV

WHY?

Sometimes, Father, I'm like a child. I want to know why. But, like a wise Father, You don't always give an answer. You know that, with my human understanding, I can't comprehend Your sovereign ways or grasp the purpose of Your decisions. So You withhold some information from me because it's not good for me to know. Help me be content to let You run the universe. I'll probably always ask questions, but I trust in You. So, even amid the mysteries of life, I rest assured, secured, and adored, knowing You mean the best for me. Amen.

"The secret things belong to the Lord our God, but those things which are revealed belong to us and to our children forever."
Deuteronomy 29:29 NKJV

DETOUR AHEAD!

Dear God, the road of my life suddenly detoured! I'm on a path I didn't bargain for. This wasn't in the plan I made for my future. What are You doing in my life, Lord? I'm Your child. I've tried to put You first; I've served You. So why is this happening? I don't understand how this could possibly be a positive thing for me. It makes no sense. Please bless me with perseverance and patience while I wait for You to show me what's next. Amen.

Moreover we know that to those who love God, who are called according to his plan, everything that happens fits into a pattern for good.
ROMANS 8:28 PHILLIPS

HELP IN TEMPTATION

Lord, I'm facing temptation in my life. I know it's not from You, because the Bible tells us that You don't tempt anyone (see James 1:13). That means it's from Satan, who definitely does not have my welfare in mind. He tempts us with things that look good on the outside but are rotten on the inside. Help me remember that Satan is a deceiver, a liar. Provide the way of escape that You promised. And let me have victory through the blood of Christ. Amen.

No temptation has overtaken you except such as is common to man; but God is faithful, who will not allow you to be tempted beyond what you are able, but with the temptation will also make the way of escape, that you may be able to bear it.
1 CORINTHIANS 10:13 NKJV

WONDERINGS
ABOUT NEW LIFE

Dear Father, if the fruit of the womb is Your reward (see Psalm 127:3), why do women who long to have a baby have difficulty getting pregnant, whereas many who don't want a child conceive easily? Infertility is such a private but excruciating grief. Many lovely couples cannot have a child. Yet there are countless unwanted pregnancies. This is one of those things I don't understand, but I trust that You have a grand plan, and it's a good one. Let me leave it at that. Amen.

The spirit of God hath made me, and the breath of the Almighty hath given me life.
JOB 33:4 KJV

CONFIDENCE IN THESE DAYS

Dear Lord, are we in the last days? Older saints believe we are. Preachers warn us that You are coming soon. Eschatologists believe prophecy is being fulfilled with every disaster and international incident. The Bible says these kinds of things are like signs, like labor pains are a signal that birth is near. But Your Word also says no one knows when the end will come (see Mark 13:32). So, Lord, take away my worry about the end-times, keep me balanced, and help me to trust. In Jesus' name, amen.

Do not be afraid of sudden terror, nor of trouble from the wicked when it comes; for the LORD will be your confidence.
PROVERBS 3:25-26 NKJV

FIERY TRIALS

Father, I'm in the fire. Spiritually. I guess that's nothing new for Christians. I've read about saints of the past who were put in literal fires for their faith, and I've heard the testimonies of others before me who went through the furnace of testing. I know the purpose of fire is to purify; Job said that after his time of testing he would emerge as gold (see Job 23:10). I need to hold on to that as I stand here in the heat, trying to sense Your nearness and praying I'll survive. Thank You, Lord, for never leaving me. Amen.

I beg you not to be unduly alarmed at the fiery ordeals which come to test your faith, as though this were some abnormal experience.
1 PETER 4:12 PHILLIPS

MYSTERIES

Dear Lord, like many others, I'm fascinated by mysteries—I like to read them, watch them, and hear about them. The Bible tells me that You have mysteries—such as the wonder of the Incarnation, and the covenant relationship between a husband and wife representing Christ and the Church. In an earthly story the mystery is often explained at the end of the book. Maybe someday in heaven I'll understand these mysteries; but for now, I leave them safely with You. Amen.

But we speak the wisdom of God in a mystery, the hidden wisdom which God ordained before the ages for our glory.
1 CORINTHIANS 2:7 NKJV

Father God, sometimes I wish I could see the future, but other times I'm glad I cannot. I doubt that knowing what is going to happen, and when, would make life any easier. So teach me to focus on today, on this moment. Help me to put my worries and anxieties in Your hands and to leave the future to the One who determines it. In Christ's name, amen.

"It is not for you to know times or seasons which the Father has put in His own authority."
ACTS 1:7 NKJV

Good and Perfect Gifts

Every good and perfect gift is from above, coming down from the Father of the heavenly lights.

James 1:17 NIV

PRECIOUS PROMISES

The Bible is full of Your promises, Lord. There is one for every event, emotion, and season of my life. Believers of every age have stood firm on these promises and had the strength to weather temptation, face persecution, endure grief, and triumph over every obstacle they encountered. Thank You for filling the pages of scripture with such beautiful assurances of Your presence and power. It blesses me to know I can turn to them in times of need. Amen.

He has given us his very great and precious promises.
2 PETER 1:4 NIV

CONVENIENCE IS A GIFT

Dear Lord, I am so glad for modern conveniences—especially dishwashers and washing machines. Women in days past spent a significant amount of time cleaning dishes and clothing—the hard way. If I had to do that plus keep up with my schedule, I'd never make it. I'm sure there were benefits to doing all that by hand, but I wouldn't want to trade places. The olden days sound romantic in some ways, but when it comes to housework, give me the twenty-first century. Thank You for every mechanical blessing You've given me, God. Amen.

Every man should eat and drink and enjoy the good of all his labor—it is the gift of God.
ECCLESIASTES 3:13 NKJV

MEMORIES

Thank You, heavenly Father, for giving me the ability to recall happy times from the past. No one can ever take those memories away from me. The moments and emotions stored in my mind can't be dumped into the "recycle bin" or erased from the disc by someone else. Memories define us and sometimes give us the inspiration to continue on. I'm grateful to have so many happy ones. Amen.

"Let them show the former things, what they were, that we may consider them, and know the latter end of them."
ISAIAH 41:22 NKJV

MESSENGERS AND WARRIORS

Dear Lord, thank You for angels—Your messengers and warriors. The stories of those who've encountered these heavenly beings fascinate me. I wonder if I've ever met an angel and didn't know it? You have a vast host of angels at Your command and often dispatch them for our good. Yet, on the cross, You did not call them to Your own aid. Instead, You willingly gave Your life for me, and now the angels want to understand that kind of love. How awesome is Your amazing love for a woman like me. Amen.

Even angels long to look into these things.
1 PETER 1:12 NIV

COFFEE AND CHOCOLATE!

God, thank You for chocolate and coffee! You are the mastermind behind the creation of cocoa and coffee beans, as well as cream, milk, sugar, and flavor shots. You let humankind discover the wonderful combinations they all make. Help me to practice discipline when I indulge in these tasty pleasures; help me not to be a glutton. And let me remember that chocolate and coffee are only treats, not a fix for my problems. But I plan to praise You every time I savor a taste of these incredible indulgences—in appropriate portions of course. Amen!

*Therefore do not let anyone judge
you by what you eat or drink.*
COLOSSIANS 2:16 NIV

THE BLISS OF HOME

Father in heaven, all across the nation, there are homeless people living on the streets or in the forests. Yet a "home" is so much more than the structure and furnishings. It's an aura, a frame of mind, a feeling of comfort, a place to rest secure. No matter where I am physically, Lord, my true home is where You are, for I am but a sojourner in this world. Thank You for being my permanent refuge, the principal resident of my happy home. Amen.

May Christ through your faith [actually] dwell (settle down, abide, make His permanent home) in your hearts! May you be rooted deep in love and founded securely on love.
EPHESIANS 3:17 AMP

SENSORY JOYS

Dear God, thank You for the five senses—sight, sound, touch, smell, and taste. You could have designed a virtual world, but instead You created one that can be experienced. Today I want to revel in the fact that I'm alive. I want to delight in the tactile joys I often take for granted. I'm grateful for each one. Amen.

For in him we live, and move,
and have our being.
ACTS 17:28 KJV

GENDER IS A BLESSING

Father God, You chose our gender for us for a purpose. Even though my hormones go haywire during pregnancy, menopause, or other monthly events, I do thank You for making me a woman. Help me to live out before a watching world the contentment to be found in accepting Your gift of womanhood and all the perks that sometimes go with it. Amen.

So God created man in His own image; in the image of God He created him; male and female He created them.
GENESIS 1:27 NKJV

ANIMAL FRIENDS

Thank You for creating the animals in our world. Though they aren't on the same value scale as humans, they are a wonderful testament to Your love for living things, and they bring glory to You just by being what they are. Help me always to be kind to the animals You have given us. May I be a good caretaker of Your property. Thank You for not only pets but the wild creatures as well. Amen.

"For You created all things, and by Your will they exist and were created."
REVELATION 4:11 NKJV